Alice M Ball

**Buttercups and Clover**

Alice M Ball

**Buttercups and Clover**

ISBN/EAN: 9783337422745

Printed in Europe, USA, Canada, Australia, Japan

Cover: Foto ©Lupo / pixelio.de

More available books at **www.hansebooks.com**

# BUTTERCUPS AND CLOVER.

BY

ALICE M. BALL.

Far richer flowers, abloom a stately stem,
  With fair birds hovering over,
Cannot conceal or crowd from haunts of men
  Our buttercups and clover.

––––––––

OFFICE OF
TRIUMPHS OF FAITH.
BUFFALO, N. Y.
1885.

BAKER, JONES & CO.,
*Printers and Bookbinders.*
BUFFALO, N. Y.

# PREFACE.

——

THE little ballads contained in this volume are
nothing more than their name declares, com-
monplace blossoms that will by no means compare
favorably with loftier flowers of brighter hue.
Some of them have previously appeared in print,
and others are given to the public for the first time.
Some are written with special reference to the
author's little friends.

They are the spontaneous outburst of a heart
that *longed* to sing, but whose earliest warblings,
because of great physical prostration and its conse-
quent privations ere the threshold of the twelfth
birthday had been reached, were attuned to a minor
key.  If towards the close of this little volume the
reader is able to detect the more exultant notes of

joy and gladness which thrilled the heart as the lines were written, to Him who so wondrously liberates and restores, she would ascribe all the praise.

A. M. B.

PITTSFIELD, MASS., Jan. 28, 1885.

# CONTENTS.

# BUTTERCUPS AND CLOVER.

# ONWARD.

ONE by one our days are speeding onward,
    Summer is past and autumn fairly here;
One by one, however gay and gladsome
    They may have bloomed, spring beauties disap-
    pear.

One by one the leaves that clung so closely
    To parent stems, are fluttering down to death;
While one by one geraniums and pansies,
    Sweet and bright-eyed, are yielding up their
    breath.

One by one the birds that sang so sweetly,
    And reared their young in our tall trees, have
    flown;

One by one night shadows gather thickly,

    Where, not long since, the noonday sun has

        shone.

One by one—how can my pen portray it?—

    The grief that gathers where the death-shades

        fall,—

Voices are hushed and loved forms disappearing:

    Change and decay are written, sore, for all.

One by one the days are speeding onward,

    And we rejoice to mount them and away

To that fair clime where Christ, our life, assures us

    We reign with Him through an eternal day.

One by one our duties rise before us,

    And, like our days, soon pass beyond recall;

Be these fulfilled, that thus our hearts be rescued

    From vain regret, when we have passed them all.

# THE OLD SCHOOL-HOUSE.

WERE it not for Hope's transplendent beams
    I might be sad to-day;
I cannot forget, as I journey on, some scenes that
    have passed away;
Fond memory lifts a mystic veil, I glance adown
    the years
That have filled my life-cup thus far up—across
    some dark with tears—
    At a snug little school-house, brown and bare,
    At a group of children collected there.

Such happy children! it sometimes seems I shall
    hear their laughter soon,
And catch the sound of the furnace bell that told
    the hour of noon;

I count the pairs of eager eyes—they are black and

blue and grey,

And farther on the dinner-pails that stood in bright

array;

And see the dense shade of the pleasant wood

That skirted the plain where the school-house

stood.


I long to skip the broad lapse of years that blurs

my picture land,

To leave for a moment these elder folk, amidst

which group I stand,

And join again my childhood mates; I often wish I

knew

Concerning their further journey on and the paths

that each pursue.

Have they learned, I wonder, to work and wait

For the uplifting of Zion's gate?

I long sometimes from this silent room to search
    through the crowded street
For the children I played with on the green, the
    forms I used to meet;
They are gone, all gone; I should find instead some
    men grown stern and brave,
A matron with family cares, perhaps, and here and
    there a grave.
    There have been hard lessons—an ample store,
    To be learned this side of that school-house
        door.

An old, old story is told again in the song I sing
    to-night,
There is not a day devoid of clouds, skies are not
    always bright.

The flowers I saw my schoolmates glean lay far
    beyond my reach,
But I have learned by blighted leaves the truths
    such always teach:
    That earthly bliss is a transient toy,
    That Christ alone can give us joy.

# FRIENDSHIP.

IN the bright mellow light of October,
   In a room where real sunbeams are few,
With the pillows of comfort around me,
   My dear friends, I am dreaming of you.
Fondly dreaming; the waves of remembrance
   That are gently astir in my breast,
I will crest with the foam of affection,
   And send them away to the West.


If only my thoughts in their fleetness
   Could bear me as swiftly along,
I should not be vainly attempting
   To thus pour my soul into song.

Within the enclosure of weakness,

　　I must touch not the pen of regret,

But beckon each gleam of contentment,

　　And write on each sorrow, " forget."


I live in the light of my morning,

　　Ah, woefully weary of pain;

In the path that pursueth the future;

　　Will rest ever greet me again ?

Sweet Hope, my dear friends, with fair pinions,

　　Delights to hold ever in view,—

What makes my heart glad in its sadness,

　　The hope of a visit from you.


My room is my world well encompassed,

　　My chair is my home for all time,

Neither pomp nor "goddess of fashion "

　　Rules this little kingdom of mine.

Here I wait, while the light of the morning

   Fades slowly away at my feet,

But Faith will brighten the evening,

   And Peace will lull me asleep.


Yes, I wait while the hand of the Master

   Is cleansing my soul of its sin,

O, may it, like gold from the furnace,

   Be rendered as perfect to Him.

I have read that those diamonds whose lustre

   Have in crowns unsurpassingly shone

Were the ones that in times of refining

   Have been held very close to the stone.


Within the grim circle of weakness,

   Which the chains of disease firmly hold,

I pray for the peace that God promised

   Those whom they imprisoned of old.

2

My dear friends, please hold very sacred,

 Though crowded your heart-rooms may be,

One tiny, bright spot in the corner,

 Just that in remembrance of me.

OCTOBER 19, 1874.

# HOUSE-CLEANING TIME.

O FEARFUL hours, when turmoil reigns
    complete,
When woman's mission no longer is discussed,
When dire confusion with relentless feet,
    Turns all our comfort into clouds of dust;
When timid man ne'er dares to venture home,
    And, unprotected, meet the rising vim,
When e'en the house dog wanders off alone,
    There is no safety 'neath the roof for him.

O, dreadful hours, when every inmost nook
    Is robbed of stool, or stand, or chair;
(And yet, wherever mortal eyes may look,
    Behold a grand collection there!)

Just at that hour when hungry palates wait,

   Till soap and paint fulfill their mission well,

Unlooked-for guests, from some far distant State,

   With plenteous equipments, sound your bell.


Whirlpools of coal dust, dust of every hue,

   Cloud the domestic sky;

Making the housewife's how d' do

   Seem fainter than good by.

Ah ! men may argue o'er the social pipe,

   Of women's trivial cares;

Who says her labor on life's field is light?

   Let any one who dares.


Yea, man and beast may well vacate that field,

   Where women, semi-yearly, meet this storm;

None but a woman could thus bravely face

   The dire confusion of HOUSE CLEANING born.

O! blissful hours, when quiet reigns again,

  When man and beast and timid people learn

That to those rooms where wildest chaos came,

  They may in safety once again return.

# OUR TWILIGHT TALK.

THE sunshine had fled from the valley,
  The sky was ablaze in the west,
When two very tiny white figures,
  Who oft, before going to rest,
Beseech for a story and kisses,
  Begged now the same favors of me,
The gifts that are seldom withholden,
  Where love has control of the key.

I covered the rose-lips with kisses,
  Receiving my share in return;
When auntie was coaxed for a story
  By those who are eager to learn

What sort of a world they have entered;

    If it is as nice as it seems,

To find one's self living and sporting

    With courage and gladness and dreams.

I told them the story of David,

    Who slew a great man with a sling.

I told them God cares for the children,

    And then bade these little ones sing.

We sang the sweet song—grown familiar—

    "When Jesus was here among men";

Said Harold, aside, in soft accents:

    "I would like to have been with them then."

When Arnold, the elder, reproving,

    The wish that was offered in vain,

Began the first words of the verses,

    And asked us to sing them again,

We sang, with no more interruption,

   The hymn from beginning to close,

Then with his hands dropped in his pocket,

   Our Harold began to "suppose."


"Suppose," said he, "I had been David,

   Had killed that great man with a stone,

You would have been greatly astonished,

   At what a small urchin had done."

I explained to impetuous Harold,

   That David was called to *obey*,

That truly *obedient* children

   Are just as courageous to-day.


That he who, through Christ, rules his spirit,

   Has slain a Goliath—take heed!—

Has gained through this Saviour of David's

   A notable triumph indeed.

The dear ones were thoughtful a moment,

Then with these old pictures in sight,

We sang a short praise song together,

And bade one another good night.

# WHAT OF THE NIGHT?

WHEN life's last day is drifting toward that
    portal
Beyond which rises all the vast unknown;
When truth, unveiled, mysteriously immortal,
    Is to the startled, eager vision shown;
When all the years that in their swift succession
    Have spanned our life, are swept into the past;
When but an hour of time, our last possession,
    Reveals its moments, quivering from our grasp;

In that dread hour, when nearing the solution
    Of life's great problems, yet unsolved by men,
Beyond the rite of faith's sublime ablution,—
    What can avail as staff of comfort then?

Naught save the knowledge, although oft mistaken

    Our steps have been, as crooked by-paths show,

Distressed, despised, by many a friend forsaken,

    Our aim has been to walk with God below.


Can souls regret when earthly hope has perished,

    And all of life seems crumbling into dust,

That earthly love, however fondly cherished,

    Was not allowed to overcome our trust?

When life's last day is drifting toward that portal

    Where darksome doubt forevermore shall cease,

May it be mine to reap the fruit immortal,

    That springs from trust, obedience and peace.

# TRUSTING.

TRUSTING, O my Father, trusting,
  In the midst of conflict wild,
In the midst of tribulation,
  Precious Lord, behold Thy child,
Bringing for Thy benediction
  Soul and body sin defiled.

Waiting, O my Father, waiting,
  (Thou hast promised) for relief
From the scourge of sin's besetments,
  From the shafts of unbelief;
Into realms of sweet submission,
  Where life's heaviest storms are brief.

Knowing, O my Father, knowing,

That Thy blessed word is true,

And Thou sayest to Thy children,

"These are written unto you."*

"Unto every soul believing,

As I promise I will do."


Trusting, waiting, O my Father,

With the knowledge, glad, sublime,

That while heaven and earth remaineth

Not one word can fail of Thine;

Bind us ever nearer to Thee,

By the cords of *truth divine.*

*John xx, 31.

# QUESTIONS.

WHERE is the life, however closely bound
    And burdened with the weary weight of
  pain,
But may have some rich stores of knowledge found,
    That for the world it would not lose again?

Where is the life cheered onward by the truth,
    The solid truth that ever guides aright,
The aged Christian of Christ-loving youth,
    That does not hold a thankful heart to-night?

Where is the soul, whose hope is firmly stayed
    On Christ, the source of purity and light,

That is not grateful for the progress made

    Towards truths that live and evermore grow

        bright?


Full many a heart has learned through Christ to

    bear

    A heavy grief with silent lips for years;

Full many a heart in sorrow—even there—

    Finds cause more for rejoicing than for tears.

# WEALTH.

I HAVE great wealth, but not in goods that tar-
nish and decay,
Not in the currency retained by eager hands to-day;
I have no gold to gather dust, to guard with jeal-
ous eye,
No bank o'er whose deposits heirs may quarrel
when I die.

Nor does my wealth consist of bonds that govern-
ments sustain,
I have no real estate to be despoiled by drouth or
rain;
The wealth of which my soul now boasts has no
metallic glow,
But it consists of hidden gems amidst the hearts
I know.

Ah! the possessions which I claim, of which my
life has need,

Lie in the knowledge *I have friends*, and I *am* rich
indeed,

In the glad knowledge that our Lord is taking care
of me,

Preparing on beyond a home for all eternity.


My bonds are each sustained of God, my kingdom
is above,

But great possessions I have gained among the
hearts I love;

And I have wealth, abundant wealth, for my joy
has been given,

Warm loving hearts, friends here below, and treasures great in heaven.

3

# BESSIE AND HER PETS.

IN a clean and cosy corner
  Of the hay mow in the barn,
'Midst the fragrance of dried clover,
  The aroma of the farm,
Four white puffy balls—four kittens—
  Cuddle in the hay;
Dot and Dimple we have named them,—
  Frost and Snow, in May.

Dot has pretty spots of blackness
  Near each tiny pink-tipped ear,
While on either cheek, believe me,
  Dimple's cunning spots appear.

Frost and Snow, in spotless whiteness,

In the center roll,

While old Mother Puss serenely

Superintends the whole.


Baby Bess, this early morning,

Seated on a mossy log,

Thinking of this nest of kittens,

Said to Skelterheels, her dog,

"There are pussies in the hay mow;

Come and let us see

What these babies and their mamma'

Think of you and me."


Skelter seemed far more than willing,

And in raptures tried to say,

"Naught could give me greater pleasure

Than a call on cats to-day."

So they trudged demurely forward,
  Innocent and sweet,
Bessie talking of the welcome
  Doggie was to meet.

" Pussy, I have come with Skelter,"
  Little Bess began to say;
Without further ceremony
  Madam Pussy cleared the way.
O'er the little maiden's bonnet;
  Skelter, at the door,
Made apologies for calling,
  Loud and deep and sore.

Hour of twilight—Bess and Skelter,
  Sitting in the shade,
Take review of late disaster,
  The mistake they made.

Bess thinks Puss was vexed at Skelter,

　That he dared to call

Till she issued invitations'

　To the dogs and all.

# AN EASTER SONG.

LITTLE children, Easter dawneth,
    Easter morn in roseate hue,
Breaks with resurrection promise,
    Brings a message, dears, to you.
Little children, Easter dawneth—
    Haste from slumbrous realms away;
He who died for little children
    Has arisen, lives to-day.
        Harken! Easter bells are ringing,
        And gay plumaged birds are singing,
        While the children's hands are bringing
        Flowers to deck the cross.

There can be no time as joyous
  As this lovely Easter morn,
Save the festive Christmas season,
  When the Holy Child was born.
And resplendent with the glory
  Of the resurrection joy,
Childish lips repeat the story,
  Dear to every girl and boy,
Of the love wherewith the Saviour,
  King, Almighty Sovereign, He
Said in sweetest condescension,
  "Bring the little ones to Me."

And He lives, He reigns forever,
  Prince of peace, the children's Friend,
Opening doors on Easter morning
  Into worlds that never end.

Harken! Easter bells are ringing,

Easter carols hearts are singing,

While the children's hands are bringing

Flowers to deck the cross.


Ever upward, blessed Master,

From the depths below,

Guide the little ones that seek thee,

Lead the tender lambs that love thee,

Into Easter glow.

# OUR OLD HOME.

TO SISTER E—.

I AM often fondly dreaming of our home upon
the hill,

Within that dear old farm-house fond memories
linger still,

Where katydids made music through many a sum-
mer day,

While you sang happy sonnets, and I rejoiced in
play.

Ours was no stately mansion, but a bright and
roomy nest,

Which, since it held our treasures, seemed of all
homes the best;

There is no brighter kingdom, thus we were taught
 to sing,

Than home when love has entered, and freely cho-
 sen king.


Around us spacious meadows displayed their emer-
 ald green,

Broad, beauteous strips of verdure, with flowing
 brooks between;

While sweetest music, surely, which brooks pre-
 sume to sing,

Went gurgling past our windows in early days of
 spring.


There were no grand equipments in that snug mid-
 dle room,

Where in the midst of winter we culled the sweets
 of June.

Our carpet was not brussels, but every bit as
dear,

And mother planned the filling for new ones every
year.

In this room father told us the stories of his youth,

And proved to us the beauty of honor, love and
truth,

While mother deftly taught us to prize the goodly
pearls

Of purity and patience, which she bequeathed her
girls.

Those days were full of brightness, we seldom
dreamed of clouds,

Robed in the garb of gladness, where were the
need of shrouds?

We thought life's hardest lessons our schoolmaster
unfurled,
And no ruler grim save "Greenleaf" in all God's
boundless world.

Those days have long since vanished, our joy was
broken soon,
And we have learned that sorrow may shroud the
skies in June;
I wield the pen now sadly and darken what was
fair,
By lingering in silence by father's vacant chair.

O home! where is your brightness when father's
smile is gone?
Its fairest scenes are blighted since mother walks
alone.

That gleeful little maiden, who so rejoiced in play,

Has left her dolls for duties she may not shirk

to-day.

# ROBIN'S TRIALS.

NOT far away from our wide open door,
 Which children's laughter filled,
Deftly and well, if puss would sin no more,
 A robin planned to build.
A cosy nook is the one place she chose,
 A tree's low crotch, rich apple bloom among,
And here she hoped in snugness and repose
 To brood and rear most tenderly her young.

With cunning skill, by tender branches held,
 The tiny floor was laid,
While from our door young eager eyes beheld
 How robin's nest was made.

Through all the morn the birdies to and fro,

    Their love intense, their thought of danger none,

Failed to observe, in sly nooks just below,

    A crafty cat, sure to besiege their home.


O busy builders ! beauteous is the spot

    Where you delight to stay,

But I in love, though you believe it not,

    Must tear your nest away.

Thus mamma said, then kindly interfered

    To save these birdies sharper, deeper pain,

Tore into bits the home so neatly reared,

    Advising birds ne'er to build low again.


Cruel indeed must robin think the hand

    That thus destroys her home,

Averted pain she cannot understand,

    Sweet charity has none.

Dear little readers, to this truth attend,

  Full many a one o'er dire disaster cries,

Because unable now to comprehend

  That love, sincere, comes often in disguise.

# A COUNTY SONG.

BELOVED Berkshire !
　Quite unsurpassed for lovely valley views,
And beauteous range of hills, thou surely art
Touched by a brush dipped in autumnal hues,
　Thou dost, indeed, quite captivate the heart.

Above thy compeers, as fond nature flings
　Reflected glow o'er wooded hill and dale,
We claim thee Queen, while harvest halo brings
　And o'er thy beauty spreads a mystic veil.

We love thy fame, and fondly boast of toil
　Long since endured, by sires gone back to dust,
To freely purge from our New England soil
　That which defiles and causeth souls to rust.

4

O that the gems of purity divine,

    Implanted here in ages that are gone,

Midst Berkshire hills may never cease to shine—

    Within our vales—continue on and on.


Here in our midst, hearts loyal to the truth,

    Be our one aim, or progress counteth naught,

Tall glimmering spires, with dissipated youth,

    Disgrace the land for which our fathers fought.


Berkshire, beloved, ne'er be it said of thee,

    Thou art stiff-necked since thou art waxen strong,

Beyond the glow of thy prosperity

    A love exists that waits and suffereth long.

# THE STOLEN NEST.

THE trees are abloom in the orchard;
    The daisies, a thousand and one,
With dew drops that sparkle like diamonds,
    Are nodding their heads in the sun.
While in the deep shade of a pear tree,
    Too sorry and frightened to play,
An urchin, ashamed and bewildered,
    This morning has hidden away.

I wonder if you, little people,
    Can guess the real cause of his shame,
Can tell why the boy is unwilling
    To tell me his home or his name?

"Ah yes," cries a bright-eyed young maiden,

"I think he has done something wrong,

And so does not wish you to mention

A name so disgraced in your song."


A nest from yon tree he has stolen,

Which the birdies worked hard to complete,

And in it were four little robins,

So helpless, and tender and sweet!

No wonder he hides in the shadows,

Ashamed of the deed he has done, .

Away from his merry companions,

Away from the light of the sun.


He is worse than the thief who plundered

Our father's coat pocket of gold,

The robber who entered our household,

So dreadfully saucy and bold.

For far above gold and its treasures,

   We prize our loved ones in the nest;

And the villain who plundered our parlor

   Ne'er stole mother's babes from her breast.


Then what shall we say of the monster

   Who robs the sweet birds of their own?

Who spoils what they labor to finish,

   Their wonderful snug little home?

Is it strange that the boy in the orchard

   Is burdened with sorrow and shame?

We will leave him in shadow and silence,

   And not even *ask* him his name.

# DEATH OF SANTA CLAUS.

IT was a cold night in winter,
　　And the snow was very deep,
All the trees stood grim and leafless,
　　As if nature were asleep;
While Jack Frost through every crevice
　　Seemed intently bound to creep.

I lay, little readers, dozing,
　　With my book beside the bed,
Thinking of the Christmas stories
　　I had but that evening read.
When I dreamed somebody whispered :
　　" Dear old Santa Claus is dead."

I was but a tiny maiden,

    I awoke right out of sleep,

And ran with my grievous burden

    To my mother's lap to weep.

And she smiled when I prayed Jesus

    Dear old Santa's soul to keep.

Then she told me, very sweetly,

    What she thought her child should know,

There was never a *real* Santa,

    We had just imagined so,

And kind friends had, Christmas morning,

    Filled our stockings, dears, you know.

Then I wept with heartfelt sorrow,

    As I knelt beside my bed,

"You will lose friends more substantial

    Than old Santa," mother said,

"Friends whose work will not continue
Just as well when they are dead."

Since I buried old St. Nicholas
Out beneath an unknown sea,
I have found things quite as shallow,
As old Santa proved to be;
There are hearts that prove as fickle
As old Santa did to me.

Little children, hear my story,
For I am not nearly through,
Until I have said that *Jesus*
Is a Friend *abiding*, *true;*
One who loves us all most dearly,
Even little ones like you.

Over Him the star of Bethlehem

   Rose above the shades of night,

Over him the Christmas morning

   Broke with a triumphant light;

And our lives are crowned with gladness

   Since the Christian's hopes are bright.

# TRUST AND BE STILL.

KNEEL close beside my couch, mamma,
   And tell me, if you know,
Why my life's brightness fled so soon,
   Why sorrow veils it so?
This world seemed very fair to me,
   Like a delightsome home;
My heart was buoyant with its hopes;
   Why must this change need come?

Thus moaned a disappointed heart,
   A maiden young and fair,
Who, to a dense shade borne apart,
   Was called to suffer there.

"Know this, my child;" that mother plead
  For grace with every breath;
Grace that gave Abram strength to guide
  His only son to death;
" Know this, my child, a 'need be' lies
  Concealed within the cloud,
And the same hand that chastens may
  Some greater peril shroud.
I have been told a story, dear,
  It may, or not, be true,
Which, since it solaced me to hear,
 * I will repeat to you.


"Two painters side by side had toiled
  Long o'er their works of art,
Till, gladdened by that grand success
  Dear to the artist's heart,

One straightway paused, and stepping back,
　　Gazed on his work the while,
With pride exultant in his heart,
　　With victory in his smile.
Back o'er the narrow scaffold, till
　　But one step more was death,
When his companion, looking up,
　　With fear suspended breath,
With wisdom that made torture gain,
　　O'er the friend's canvas fair,
Swept a swift, broad, destructive hand,
　　That left its impress there.
Shocked beyond measure by the deed,
　　By the destruction wrought,
The man rushed forward—life was saved—
　　The friend gained what he sought.

" When o'er our pictures, dear, a Hand

    Sweeps all the light away,

When hopes we cherish, treasures gained,

    Fade in a single day;

Know then, my child, some 'need be' lies

    Concealed beneath the ill;

Since He who chastens knows and loves,

    We'll trust Him and 'be still.' "

# ANOTHER YEAR.

ANOTHER year for Jesus,
  Is added to those years,
With their bright days and darksome,
  Their sunny spots and tears,
That towards time's wondrous vortex
  Are drifting swift and deep;
Another year, dear Master,
  For Thee to guard and keep.


Another year for Jesus,
  Another scroll of time,
With blurred and sin-stained pages,
  For those dear hands of Thine,

To turn with tender pity,

    When books have been unsealed,

Wherein truth is recorded,

    And all things are revealed.


Another year, good Master,

    Thou has granted us below,

Wherein to heed Thy counsel,

    Accept Thy love and grow;

For some a year of gladness,

    Thy healing voice is heard,

Dispelling worlds of thraldom

    By the magic of Thy word.


Another year of watching,

    For many a weary soul;

Another year of waiting,

    Ere the Master maketh whole.

For some a year of hardship,

A weary round of care;

For others, one of triumph,

'Tis thus, Lord, everywhere.


In faith we are receivers,

In discipleship Thine own;

Called to be saints and soldiers,

Called to be pilgrims lone,

Called to be friends, not servants,

Of Christ, our Priest and King;

Called to be heirs with Jesus,

Our hearts rejoice and sing.


We humbly ask, dear Master,

That our New Year's gift may be,

All meaner things forsaking,

Rich fellowship with Thee.

Our hearts at rest and tranquil,
  Thy blessed will our own,
Until we know Thee fully
  In Thy eternal home.

# THE BABE OF BETHLEHEM.

DEAR little children there was once a babe
    So fair, so pure, methinks the angels smiled
Above the spot where'er the babe was laid,
    While beauteous peace shed halos o'er the child.

We only know He came to us divine,
    This wondrous babe, whom prophets had foretold,
With hands and feet and lips, dear ones, like thine,
    To guide, to guard from evil, and grow old.

We do not know if Christ, the Master, wore
    What you would style a long and beauteous dress,
But we are sure no babe appeared in more
    Real regal robes of radiant righteousness.

We love to read of Simeon's love and praise,

   As he beheld the infant child divine;

We wonder if, in any of its ways,

   Our babyhood was like this—yours and mine.


We love to read and think about the star

   That, all resplendent, o'er this child arose;

That lit and led the wise men from afar,

   From gardens, halls, to love's lowly repose.


Sometimes we seem to see Him as he grew

   From babyhood into maturer years,

This strange, shy child, that no one ever knew,

   Save those, through faith, to whom the light ap-

      pears.


And when drew near the yearly paschal feast,

   Whereat this boy first met the learned men,

(Doctors divine and wise men from the east

    Met once a year to keep Passover then).


We think that He in quiet grandeur passed

    Within the Temple at His parents' side,

And, doubtless, with a candor unsurpassed,

    Harkened to much His purity denied.


Passover ended, as all homeward bound,

    Were those whom Christ's fond parents were

        among,

The boy brought with them could nowhere be

        found—

    The blessed Christ-child was no longer young.


Amidst the doctors and the learned men

    They found their son, those parents in dismay,

And doubtless saw the work beginning then

˙ O'er which our hearts grow rapturous to-day.


You know the story, little children, well,

   The Babe of Bethlehem is now Christ, the King;

His wondrous love and sweet obedience tell,

   While we his never-ceasing praises sing.

# A PLEA IN BEHALF OF LADIES' TEMPERANCE UNION.

WE plead with those whose homes are
    bright,
  For those who sit in gloom,
From darksome doors we turn to yours,
  With light and love abloom,
And plead for those throughout our land,
  Wives, mothers, sisters, friends,
Who tremblingly espy a foe
  From which no law defends.

We come with pity in our hearts
  For fallen, fellow-men;
We bring grieved mothers and their babes,
  And gently plead for them.

Within their homes a subtle foe,
   Most grim design hath laid;
Shall little children, jeopardized,
   Appeal in vain for aid?


There are fond mothers in our land,
   Amidst the poor and lone,
With depths of love within their souls,
   As fervent as our own.
We hear their prayer, behold their woe,
   Until with voice and pen
We are resolved to face the storm
   And firmly ask for them.


That kind consideration, which
   Hearts loyal, heaven born,
Will render those who at their side
   Lie bruised and crushed and torn.

We plead with Heaven, we plead with men;
    God overrules the whole,
But ne'er fulfills a law to save,
    Souls choose to disannul.

God speed the day when those we choose
    To represent our cause,
Those whom we know, from out the mass
    Make and enact our laws,
Shall be preferred for moral worth,
    Firm principles and true,
Not for the paltry gain, dear sir,
    That may accrue to you.

We hail with glad, exultant hearts
    Each advance step of love,
Dispelling selfish arrogance,
    Distilling from above

Kind fellow-feeling for the pangs

Within our neighbor's home,

A heart awake to others' needs

As well as these—our own.


God speed the day when temperance reigns

Triumphant in our land,

When in pursuance of the truth

Men journey hand in hand.

Until the dawn of that glad morn,

May Heaven accept the prayer;

Frail women, heart compassion stirred,

Are lifting everywhere.

# LINES WRITTEN BY REQUEST

IN BEHALF OF THE

## LADIES' AID SOCIETY,

*- AT ITS 20th ANNIVERSARY.*

M. E. CHURCH, PITTSFIELD, MASS., 1885.

WE have convened at this auspicious time,
    With grateful hearts, with trophies old
and new,
And as we meet would form ourselves in line,
Of seasons past to take a brief review.


Our aim has been, as name and deeds declare,
    To aid our church—inferior aims aside;
God's own dear Son, acknowledged Son and Heir,
Accepts the church as His appointed Bride.

Twice have we toiled through a decade of years,
  With purpose true, concerning Christ's espoused,
Amidst much change, alternate hopes and fears,
  With willing hands and energies aroused.

Oft has it been our destiny, as sheep,
  To meet with change of shepherds on our way;
Ours to behold a stranger sometimes reap
  Seeds that were scattered at an earlier day.

We would not try to cover or conceal
  .These vacant places in our ranks—deplored—
Each backward glance some broken links reveal,
  Too sadly sacred to be soon ignored.

Some from our midst, by nuptial glitter won,
  Have disappeared, and other paths pursue;

Cupid attracts, and shortly, one by one,

Our dear young ladies, *may* encompass *you*.


We love our church, of which its members hold

Allotted parts, in honor, as we trust.

May it, as type of the blest upper fold,

Prosper and grow, as God's own kingdom must.


We know the Word concerning this dear spot,

"John second sixteenth," gives it as it is;

And petty zeal of merchandise must not

Usurp the spirit in this house of His.


May it be ours to heed our Lord's commands,

Each for ourselves accept the "better part;"

And while we serve with Martha's busy hands,

Know that it is with Mary's loving heart.

A word of greeting we would tender those
   Who this large flock have guided, first and last,
Most grateful praise for what each member knows
   Of pastoral care in seasons that are past.

Endeared to us by sacredness of ties,
   That nought can mar, or disannul or break,
Is every hand that points us to the skies,
   And leads us thither for the Master's sake.

# LOST—THE SOUND OF FOOT-STEPS.

L OST, the sound of footsteps, my own footsteps; just once more

Do I long to hear the music of my feet upon the floor,

Dream I oft of days departed, when my lips first learned to talk

Of the mother-love that fondly taught a little child to walk;

In the silence that surrounds me, tired of silence, tired of pain,

Do I long for hands to guide me till I learn to walk again.

Lost, the sound of footsteps, ah! the days have
    come and gone,
And my steps, forever silenced, wake no echo in
    our home.
Music sweetly floats about me, wafted on the morn-
    ing air,
And the hum of merry voices floats about me
    everywhere.
While I fondly long for music that can be mine
    nevermore,
The glad music of my footsteps, my own footsteps
    on the floor.

Lost, the sound of footsteps, and I wait day after
    day,
In the midst of this long silence, where the Master
    bids me stay,

Dreaming of the spacious meadows where my
child feet used to roam,
Of the footprints left so often on the graveled
walks at home.
Does the Father know how restless our weak human feet may grow?
Is He guiding just as surely when they lie in shadows so?

Lost, the sound of footsteps, when the soul's work
here is done,
When the gates of heaven are opened, and the Master bids me come
From the silence so unbroken by the tread of human feet,
Over where immortal footsteps sound upon a gold-
en street.

Until then, dear Father, teach me that amidst these
fearful depths,
E'en this long unbroken silence, Thou art guiding
still my steps.
When this earthly life is ended, on beyond may I
once more
Hear the gladsome sound of footsteps, my own
footsteps on the floor.

# REGAINED—THE SOUND OF FOOTSTEPS.

AFTER these long years of waiting,
　　All these weary years of pain,
Is it I that stand firm-footed
　　Underneath clear skies again?
Can it be—O joy surpassing
　　Anything my life has known—
That within God's Holy Temple
　　Footsteps sound that are my own?

None but those who are imprisoned,
　　Sound the depths of prison gloom;
None so well when granted freedom
　　Know the sweetness of the boon.

Buds of promise long unfolding

    Oft produce the richest bloom.

Do you marvel if in gladness

    O'er the wondrous powers that be,

O'er the Saviour's loving kindness,

    So compassionate and free,

I exclaim, in tones exultant,

    Hear what Christ has done for me?

May my steps henceforth be guided

    By a Hand that is divine,

May the footprints left behind me

    On the shifting sands of time,

In obedience and mercy,

    Blessed Lord, resemble Thine.

# A CORONATION SONG.

FRESH mercies fresh oblations claim;
  Lord, at Thy feet we fall,
To pay obeisance to that name
  That crowns Thee King of all.
King, Sovereign, all superior Lord,
  Who can compare with Thee?
What match the wonders of the word
  That giveth life to me?

O for a pen wherewith to sound
  This matchless love abroad;
To speak the pleasure that is found
  By heart repose in God.

To swell the music of His word,

    Through life's most darksome days,

Till every sin-sick soul has heard

    How marvellous His ways.


Love, far surpassing human thought,

    Is the rich gift of heaven;

Love, matchless love, divinely wrought,

    And most divinely given;

Love never ceasing, wondrous, grand,

    Old, and yet ever new,

Upon a parched, sin-smitten land

    Distilling heaven's dew.


Love that sometimes by sunset skies,

    A moment is concealed,

While holy, deathless stars arise,

    And glory is revealed.

O, for a thousand tongues to swell

Our great Redeemer's praise;

A holier, purer life to tell

The wisdom of His ways.

www.ingramcontent.com/pod-product-compliance
Lightning Source LLC
Chambersburg PA
CBHW021422090426
42742CB00009B/1214